THE POWER OF RELATIONSHIPS IN PROFESSIONAL GROWTH

JEFF LERNER

This book is dedicated to all who have supported me in my career, and all who have pushed me to exceed the expectations I set for myself.

For my grandfather, who will never have a chance to read this, but always taught me the importance of relationships and the art of shaking hands.

And for Anna, who constantly reminds me to "Do Epic Shit."

Table Of Contents

INTRODUCTION

In the second season of *Orange Is the New Black,* the very successful Netflix dramedy series based on the true story of Piper Kerman, a woman who served a prison sentence for money laundering, one particular episode highlighted some truths about relationships. The episode featured the history between Red, a Russian-born inmate who controlled the prison's kitchen, and Vee, an African-American inmate who controlled most of the prison's illegal heroin trafficking. Both women clearly were the leaders of their respective groups.

Through a series of flashbacks, we learn that Red was once a frightened new arrival at the prison. Vee, on the other hand, was a criminal veteran with a firm understanding of power and relationship dynamics—especially pertaining to dealings with fellow criminals. Since the two women were to be cellmates, Vee extended an olive branch of friendship to Red, and they became friends.

Not too long afterward, Red identified a prison business opportunity. In prison, having the ability to access contraband—like cigarettes—provides one with a lot of negotiating power. As the leader of the kitchen workgroup, she was in a position to smuggle items of considerable interest into the prison population via the weekly delivery of supplies to the kitchen.

Soon, Red became the go-to person for things that inmates couldn't get on their own. She began to amass power quickly, in large part because most of the women were willing to do her bidding. Using starvation as a weapon, Red could punish anyone who crossed her, as she was in charge of the kitchen.

As Vee witnessed Red's rise to power and financial dominance, she became incensed and demanded that Red turn over the smuggling operation to her. Surprised that her friend would make such an outrageous demand, Red stood her ground, maintaining that the business was hers alone. She protested that she'd fought vigorously to build and groom it into the successful enterprise it had become, and that she would not give it up.

So, Vee had her underlings beat Red up—but not before telling her, "Your mistake is not having a backup." Red had failed to forge relationships with others who would have her back in tough situations. She thought that she could get by thanks to her power and her ability to run a successful smuggling business, but she failed to realize the importance of forming alliances with a tight network of people who would be willing go to war to help maintain her dominance and success in prison.

While prison life is very different from our day-to-day lives, many of us make the same mistake Red did—we are oblivious about the importance of relationships. We often don't notice when we have the chance to step up into leadership roles. Sometimes, we don't know how to act as a leader, how to interact with the people around us, or how to make use of the relationships we've already formed as we attempt to rise to higher places in our careers. Like Red, we're so focused on the career itself—namely, the money we could make, the places we could go, and the cars that we could drive as a result of our success—that we ignore the importance of personal relationships, which are perhaps the most important ingredient in advancing the career we desire.

We've grown accustomed to chasing money and career goals because we've learned that tangible, easily measured things are the most important things. Throughout our lives, we've been taught that when it comes to success, what can be counted or measured matters most: whether you scored well on the test, finished in first place in the debate competition, had a 4.0 grade point average, interned at three companies before graduation, and so on.

It's easy to determine whether your grades are falling, or if you're meeting your key performance indices, or whether you're getting rich. But it's not so easy to know if the relationships you're building will ultimately give your personal life and your career a boost. That sort of thing is very subjective; as a result, it's harder to pay attention to or measure. We tend to pay more attention to things we can see. Things that are superficial. Things that *other people* consider important.

It's ironic, then, that your career success is, in fact, dependent on the quality of the relationships you form and the experience you gather. There's a lot of truth to the saying, "It's not *what* you know, but *who* you know, that matters." Think about it: whenever you become aware of a job opportunity in your workplace or another organization you know about, a person you know who might be well suited to the position pops into your head. You don't think of someone you read about in an article; rather, you think of someone you know, likely someone you care about. He or she might not have been the valedictorian of his or her class or may not have graduated from college *magna cum laude*, but you remember the person because it's someone you trust—someone worthy of your recommendation.

That's simply the way life works. In fact, many high-level positions in many organizations are placed based on recommendations from management-level staff. It's true for some entry-level positions, too. Organizations often ask staff to look into their networks and recommend candidates for vacant positions. Most believe that it's better to hire someone for whom a person on staff can vouch than someone you don't know much about.

People want to offer opportunities to others that they know; with whom they've built and shared life experiences; those they trust and make them happy. At any stage of your professional career, and certainly in leadership roles, relationships are important. In fact, the ability to build good relationships with people is a leadership skill in and of itself. I worked at Google for almost a decade, and both then and since, I've seen some very smart individuals fail to advance their careers because of their inability to connect with others, show empathy and understanding, and build relationships rooted in trust.

The pioneering work of Steve Jobs and Bill Gates changed the way we live—everything from making the writing of this book much easier with a computer, to getting quick access to the vast stores of knowledge on the Internet using a phone I can take anywhere. The smartphone technology we enjoy and often take for granted was the direct result of a relationship between two smart people who wanted to change the world: in 1997, Gates invested $150 million in Apple, thus saving it from bankruptcy.

"Microsoft was the biggest software developer outside of Apple developing for the Mac," Jobs remarked. "So, it was just crazy what was happening at that time. And Apple was very weak and so I called Bill up and we tried to patch things up."

Long before Apple found itself at the brink of bankruptcy, the two industry pioneers had been friends. In the 1970s, the men collaborated on Windows and Apple projects, but eventually, conflicts in their views and vision became too great, and they went their separate ways. Gates' $150 million intervention saved Apple and allowed it to become the most valuable company in the world by 2018. So, you see: relationships make a difference, and in times of need, who you know will matter more than what you have or what you are worth, both financially and intellectually speaking.

In any organization, relationships make all the difference. Although many entrepreneurs say that product innovation and affordability—among other factors, of course—are essential to success, the truth is that relationships lie at the heart of any successful business. That's why thousands of companies spend millions of dollars on brand management, which is the practice of creating good relationships with potential and existing customers alike. No business can succeed without forming effective relationships with its customers, and sometimes even with industry competitors as well.

Relationships are, and always will be, the essence of good business. Strategies like growing social media networks and building brands are forms of corporate-level relationship management. Even in the world e-commerce, a majority of sales still take place between two human beings. Every important B2B and B2C transaction involves the participation of a buyer and seller (not to mention human-driven pre- and post-sales support). And in truth, the superior product doesn't always win; people don't always select the best or cheapest option. Purchases are driven by emotion. People buy from brands they feel a connection with. Whether in the service industry, a retail organization, or even personal finance, relationships matter.

If you take a good look at the lives of highly successful entrepreneurs, you'll find that their networks (not the social media ones—the *real* ones) are their most prized possessions. If you doubt this, pick up a favorite entrepreneur's memoir (it doesn't matter what industry). You'll find that at many defining moments, he or she leveraged his or her personal or professional relationship with another influential person to achieve a goal.

It's little wonder, then, that billionaires have other billionaires on speed dial. Have you ever wondered why some companies create exclusive clubs only their C-suite executives have access to? The short answer: relationship building. For people at that level, what matters most is who they know, so their companies actively help them build and reinforce their networks of people who can help them achieve their goals.

It's only human to fantasize about opportunities. Maybe you often find yourself daydreaming about working on a career-defining project, something that could really showcase your talents and get you noticed by upper management. Or maybe you plan to make a move to a new organization, a place where you'd feel more valued than you presently do. Or perhaps you dream about floating your own company and executing these tons of ideas that you have in your head.

But fantasies are a dime a dozen. They don't do much. What brings them to fulfillment is action through preparedness. And how can you prepare? By building relationships in the here and now. Acquire those leadership skills now—don't wait. Remember, it's never too late to start building a real network that can help you reach the goals that are now only in your dreams.

In this book, I'll walk you through every step on this path. I'll illuminate for you what actions you can take, along with real-life examples, to build and develop the relationship skills you'll need to effectively catapult yourself to the level of success you aim to achieve. Let's get started.

CHAPTER ONE

REDEFINING WHAT WE KNOW ABOUT RELATIONSHIPS

Ask yourself this question: What does career success mean to me? According to conventional definitions of the term, you'd have to reach the top of your career path in order to be considered highly successful. That means if you're not the CEO of a giant corporation, a Nobel laureate, or in possession of a highly coveted award, title, or position, you wouldn't be considered someone who has excelled professionally. This understanding of success is centered on two major assumptions. The first is that you can't be truly successful in your workplace unless you're able to climb all the way to the top. The second is that being promoted from one position to another until you reach the pinnacle of an organization is the only achievement that should matter in your professional life. But is this the way it should be?

Plenty of people who don't run multinational companies are very successful. You don't need to hold some fancy official title to be successful, or to even be viewed by others as successful. The truth is that fewer than 1 percent of the working population will ever hold these positions or titles. Does that mean the other 99 percent aren't successful? Not at all. Success isn't reserved for CEOs or senior levels of management—it's open to everyone working to improve themselves and their lifestyles. We need to shift our thinking, and replace thoughts like "I must get to the top" with a much more important question: "What really matters to me?"

That said, how *do* you measure personal and professional success? And just as important, who should be measuring it? When I think of true success, I think of a former coworker of mine at Google,

Karen Cahn. By any and all standards, Cahn was very successful; she led the growth of Google/YouTube during the video entertainment race of the 2000s (and had previously done the same at AOL). She was on the fast track, sure to rise to the top of any corporate structure, and any organization would jump at the opportunity to bring her on board.

Despite her corporate success, Cahn wanted more. Having an individual role at a media company wasn't as important to her as following her passion, so in 2016, she founded and launched iFundWomen, a crowdfunding platform based on a pay-it-forward model for startups and small businesses run by women. She made the decision to invest in herself and in her passion, rather than to focus on the success she'd achieved by anyone else's standards. Cahn had a different definition of success, and she followed her dreams to achieve it.

Belief in these traditional definitions of professional success, where we attach so much value to reaching the top, creates an assembly line of people who are frustrated by and unhappy with their professional lives. For some professionals, simply creating a plan for continued career growth is a first step to becoming successful. For others, building the relationships that will guide them on their professional journey is of the utmost importance. No matter what your goal may be, you do have a path to finding success, and it starts with that first vital question: "What really matters to me?"

On the flip side, if you view career success as a race against others, you'll quickly find yourself in a me-versus-them state of constant struggle. This kind of thinking leads some organizations to develop incentive systems focused exclusively on individuals' performance results, rather than team values, such as sharing and cooperation. While these incentives may work for some, many others prefer work environments focused on collaboration and teamwork, and they can find the same levels of success within those types of workplaces.

Stress, a challenge we all face in the workplace, can derail our path forward. Professional stress doesn't always come as a result of a heavy workload; sometimes, relationships with colleagues can be among the biggest contributors. In one of my earlier professional roles, I had a difficult relationship with my closest peer at the organization, pretty much from day one. We had different perspectives on how to move the business forward. I'd been hired to lead a specific division of the company, and he always looked for opportunities to highlight the issues my team faced—all in an attempt to make himself look better to upper management.

Instead of seeing me as a potential ally who could work with him to improve the business, he saw me as competition for advancement. Instead of feeling proud of the work I was doing, I constantly felt anxious about my long-term future at the company. I ended up leaving less than two years after I'd started there, after I found a work environment and culture better aligned with my goals. Many of us have found ourselves in "dog-eat-dog" workplaces like this, places where we have to become transactional and utilitarian instead of making genuine connections with our colleagues. We become obsessed with appearance, rather than substance, and in the process, we lose sight of what true success is.

When you think about success in your career and your life, ponder this question: If today was your last day on earth, what would you regret the most? To make the question a little easier to answer, I'll give you a few options. Will you wish that you had:

a) acquired more degrees and certifications to speed your career growth?

b) invested more money in Apple, Google, Amazon, or Microsoft?

c) spent more time with the people you care about?

Chances are that you'd pick the third option, because when we reach our final moments, career and financial success don't matter much. Deep down, we all know that maintaining strong relationships with those around us is a good thing, but we rarely make it a priority until it's too late. This is especially true of workplace relationships.

That's why it's so important to redefine what success means to you and not focus exclusively on professional titles or accolades. Instead, you should focus on building relationships, as they will help lead you to a sense of wholeness.

The first step is reevaluating the value you place on relationships. A Harvard University research project called the Grant Study, which began in the 1930s and continues to this day, sought to understand what factors contributed most to making people happy and mentally healthy. Unsurprisingly, the study found that lasting and positive relationships with the people who surround us, the people we love and respect, are the key to happiness.

The study followed 265 emotionally and physically healthy Harvard sophomores selected from the classes of 1939 to 1944 (the group included John F. Kennedy), and was also run in tandem with a second project, the Glueck Study, which followed 456 disadvantaged but non-delinquent young people from Boston selected between 1940 and 1945. All of the participants in both studies were male. The men have been evaluated at least once every two years, and those evaluations continue to this day. During the assessments, the men were asked questions about their health and their families, and how their lives have evolved over time. It found that those who had positive relationships with the people in their lives have lived longer, experienced more personal happiness, and enjoyed better physical health than those who didn't.

When I first started working at Google in New York City, at the age of 24, many of my close college friends lived nearby, so I rarely focused on building relationships with my colleagues. To my surprise, however, I soon learned that forging good relationships at the office actually improved the relationships I had in my personal life. When I went to work each day, the good relationships I had there made me feel supported, cared for, and appreciated, and this affirmation drove me to reach new heights of professional success. As my attitude toward work changed, my attitude toward life changed as well, and my friends were quick to notice. The meaningful relationships I had with my coworkers advanced both my career and my personal life considerably.

Positive relationships based on trust, respect, and love increase your life span and make you happier. Knowing you can count on the people around you, even if they don't always agree with you, gives you a sense of security. So why is this so important in the workplace as well? Because you probably spend 40 hours or more every week with your colleagues. Strong relationships there make you happier at work and also boost your productivity.

No matter how brilliant your mind or the strategies that spring from it may be, it's hard for an individual to win against a team. That's why athletes need coaches, actors need directors, students need teachers, and so on. Everywhere you go, you'll find an abundance of examples that show how working well as a team can lead to greater success than a single individual can achieve on his or her own. The same is true when it comes to nurturing a career and finding opportunities for leadership.

If you think all that you have today, as well as what you've become, are direct results of your effort alone, you need to reevaluate your professional history. Everyone who guided you down your career path, everyone who mentored you, everyone who gave you advice, everyone who introduced you to others who helped you along the way—all of these people are part of your success story. You can't live in total isolation, and you can't grow your career in isolation, either. No one does. If you want to accelerate your career and achieve your goals quickly, you'll need the help and support of other people. You'll need a team of allies and advisors, and your relationships with those people will grow over time.

People Matter

Relationships are very important to your career, no matter what type of organization you're in or what level you're at within it, because in the end, every role involves interaction with others on a daily basis. Whether you're a software developer or a project manager, at some point, you'll work closely with others. Larry Page and Sergey Brin developed the Google search function by figuring out and understanding what people wanted—and to do that, they had to talk to people. They're both extraordinarily talented individuals, of course, but they had to conduct extensive user research to better understand what needs their products could fulfill. Page and Brin talked to their friends, to business leaders, and even to complete strangers to gather feedback on their vision for Google, and much of Google's early success is due to the communication they had with people who were willing to share their perspectives and feedback. Similarly, Amazon is the mammoth that it is today because it worked hard to understand its customers and learn their pain points, and then extensively shared the data it gathered internally so the whole organization could rally behind the same goals.

So what does this all mean? It's not just technology alone that leads to success. The people behind it, and the relationships they build, are just as essential. People develop software. People write mission statements. People are at the forefront of all of the opportunities, resources, and the information you need to be successful.

People also often function as gatekeepers. Jeffrey Pfeffer, a professor of organizational behavior at Stanford University, has studied and proven that strong relationships, including staying on good terms with your immediate boss, are key to being promoted up the ladder—and has even suggested that these relationships matter more than skill or competence. In his work, Pfeffer has concluded that employees who are a little less skillful but who get along well with others and contribute more to their teams are often more valuable to a company than strong individual contributors.

These relationships are important because the people you spend time with at work eventually play a role in molding you into the person you become. The behaviors and beliefs of others—especially those of leaders we admire—are contagious. If you spend enough time around someone who's extremely punctual, before you know it, you'll begin to imitate his or her actions and absorb the trait of being punctual. If you spend enough time around someone who's very good at meeting people and starting (and maintaining) meaningful conversations with them, it's only a matter of time before you find yourself learning that skill and mimicking some of the behaviors you observed.

That relationships and teamwork are valuable is undeniable, but our culture tends to put a premium only on those people at the top. What we hear about most leading businesses is usually only focused on their leadership, rather than the teams around them. And if you read about their CEOs or other leaders in newspapers and magazines, you might walk away thinking that they reached that point in their careers because of their singular traits: grit, brains, or hard work, perhaps. Features about business leaders rarely account for the relationships they've built, despite the fact that they were key to their success.

Given that our society tends to focus on the individual, it's little wonder that books that aim to help you improve your life are tagged as "self-help," and that training programs that focus on becoming a better version of yourself are tagged as "personal development." These resources are almost entirely focused on the "me," rather than taking into account the friends, allies, mentors, and colleagues who are so integral to an individual's growth.

A simple explanation for this trend could be that the idea of being self-made simply sells better; that stories about self-made leaders make readers feel that they, too, can become a self-made success. Even the business world loves superheroes. It's much easier to tell a story about a hero than about a hero and his helpers. "Spiderman and Friends" doesn't quite roll off the tongue as easily as "Spiderman," but the hero narrative oversimplifies the truth. Every leader has benefited from a network of strong interpersonal relationships; you need to only have a one-on-one conversation with such a leader, or take a closer look into his or her life, to see evidence of this for yourself. Singlehanded success is extremely rare. Somewhere along the line, a trusted friend or colleague gave him or her advice, presented an opportunity, gave direction, provided encouragement, was willing to provide a bankroll, or offered counsel.

No one achieves success in complete isolation. It's tempting to believe that we are the heroes of our own stories, but the truth is that we are only a singular part of a large network. The cities we've lived in, the companies we've worked in, the fraternities or sororities we've joined, the families we were born into, and society at large have all provided succor and support to our careers. The people who have inspired us, helped us, counseled us, shaped us, and even hurt us, also drive us to greatness. It's impossible to separate a person from the environment in which he or she has thrived. You can't tell a true story of achievement without also providing the social context.

The whole idea of being "self-made" should be squashed into oblivion, because we all need other people to succeed. You need a team, but not just any team—you need an inner circle of people with varied strengths and abilities. Your talent and hard work may be necessary for your success, but it's not always sufficient. In the end, everything matters: your skills, your work ethic, your intelligence, and the network of the people who surround you. Your career success is dependent on your individual abilities, but also on the ability of your network to help you make the most them. Your potential for success and power increases exponentially if you have a trusted inner circle that can push you to greatness.

CHAPTER TWO

THE POWER OF THE INNER CIRCLE

If you have ever taken a Psychology 101 class, you probably learned about the work of famed psychologist Abraham Maslow. In his 1943 paper, "A Theory of Human Motivation," published in *Psychological Review*, Maslow explained what he called the "hierarchy of needs." Using a pyramid structure, Maslow explained that the most fundamental human needs—physiological necessities like shelter, food, and sleep—lie at the bottom of the hierarchy, while a need for self-actualization is at the top. There are also intermediate stages, including social needs; Maslow identified these as "love and belonging" located in the middle of the pyramid. Maslow theorized that humans need social interaction in order to survive as a species—and he was right. Truth be told, we don't just need social interaction to survive in our personal lives; we also need it to survive in our professional lives. But there's a caveat: not all social interactions are created equal.

Many believe that the bigger the network, the better. In fact, many networking gurus advise that you should grow your network as much as possible and cast the widest net. Their advice is based on the assumption that the more people you know, the more likely you are to be exposed to opportunities that can help you achieve professional goals, material success, etc. Personally, I don't think this is sound advice. Becoming a "superconnector" has nothing to do with forming a giant network; rather, it's the process of carefully curating people based on certain traits, personalities, or skills they have, and then forming an inner circle of those people. No rule says that this inner circle must include your closest colleagues, or even that they'll have similar careers to yours. Instead, the inner circle will surround you with people who share a common belief, purpose, and vision—people who know you well and are invested in seeing you achieve your professional goals. The network's size is far less important than the role each of these people will play in driving your path forward.

This is a fast-paced world, in which everyone is seemingly racing against time. You're likely caught up in work and projects—and there's this other thing, your personal life, that involves spending time with your family, friends, and loved ones. All of that leaves you very little time to network effectively. While having a large professional network entails many benefits (we'll get to that later), communicating well with a large network is almost impossible. You're left with the mass-email approach, in which you must communicate the most generic message possible in order to reach as many people as possible, and this inevitably fails to connect with anyone on a personal level.

Think about it: you're attempting to advance your career and look to others for advice or opportunities. No recipient wants to feel as though he or she is just one of hundreds (or thousands) of people who received the same message. You can bet that won't inspire someone to help you. So it's far more advantageous to invest time and energy in communicating with five or ten carefully selected people. Why overpopulate your network when you can instead create an inner circle of high-profile, influential, and smart people who can really help you become a better version of yourself?

To network correctly, you must be brutally selective. After all, the people in your inner circle are connected to others as well. For example, your curated network might include:

- **A C-suite level executive mentor.** You meet every month for discussions to help keep your vision focused on thinking big and for guidance on managing difficult professional situations.

- **A successful entrepreneur.** You get together every few weeks to gain insight and perspective on the challenges and rewards of running a small business.

- **An extended coterie of friends.** You connect with them periodically to remain cognizant of where you've come from and to stay in touch with your roots.

- **Your closest family and friends.** You spend quality time with them on the weekends to remind yourself of the significance of loyalty and caring in both your personal and professional lives.

Every conversation with inner-circle members like these can yield tremendous results. With each of these people, you will continually strengthen your bonds of trust and undiluted loyalty. You'll have free-ranging, unfiltered conversations. And you've chosen them to make up your inner circle because they make you feel like a better person and help you get closer to your goals.

Many of the most successful people in the world today have one another on speed dial. Bill Gates and Warren Buffett have been close for decades. Their relationship, which is built on mutual trust and admiration, has led to some of the greatest business successes and most significant philanthropic efforts of our generation. Actors Leonardo DiCaprio and Tobey Maguire have been friends since childhood, and they've depended on each other over the years as they've grown and refined their craft. Steve Jobs and Steve Wozniak were close friends who cofounded the tech industry behemoth Apple; eventually, they parted ways, but some of their greatest accomplishments came about thanks to their collaboration.

These three examples highlight the importance of relationships: people are willing to open doors for those whom they know and trust. Consideration for high-level career opportunities often comes about thanks to the recommendations of others, so strong relationships with coworkers, clients, and vendors are equally important to long-term professional success.

An inner circle of powerful and successful people who understand your way of thinking, can also help you identify and work on your weaknesses. Some have likely walked the same path you're on, so they can advise you about potential pitfalls along the way. They don't necessarily have to be legends in their own time; your inner circle can include those who are on the same journey with you, who are at the same point in their careers. Really, the only critical qualification is this: candidates for the inner circle must have the capacity to change your life for the better by sharing their experiences, perspective, encouragement, and guidance.

Perhaps you're considering starting a company of your own that will create a meaningful product or offer a service that solves a pressing problem—and in either case doing so profitably. Then the members of your inner circle should include at least a few people who have done the same. Industry-specific events, like networking get-togethers and conferences, are great places to meet these people. Better yet—reach out to people who are already in your network to gauge their willingness to introduce you to others in their own inner circles of trusted relationships. Connections made via people who are valued by both parties always have much more credibility than connections made at conferences or events. A stamp of approval from a trusted ally is a value that can't be matched.

As is true in any small network, figuring out who should NOT be included is almost as critical as figuring out who should. Never be afraid to distance yourself from people who don't have your best interests at heart, or from people who can't be trusted completely. Your time is valuable, so don't waste it on people who aren't helping you succeed. Instead, focus on people who:

- think clearly and innovatively;
- listen well;
- advise wisely;
- encourage strongly;
- hold you to a higher standard; and
- hold you accountable when you fail to do the right thing.

Spotting these characteristics in others involves keenly listening, in each and every conversation. Your eyes and ears should be on high alert at all times.

So How Do I Put this Network in Place?

As a first step, perform a personal self-assessment. Ask yourself the following questions, among others:

- Am I in control of my life right now, or is it being controlled by others?
- When was the last time I made a conscious effort to reach out and meet people who can help me reach my goals?
- Do I think I appear desperate at times? Why?
- Does my communications with others highlight my potential and my insights?
- Do other people seek me out or seem happy to spend time with me?

Second, assess your habits and activities. Ask yourself:

- What career-related activities have I participated in during the past two weeks? Were they worth my time?
- What would I rather invest my time and effort in doing?
- What should I stop doing altogether?
- Do I spend my time pursuing activities that align with my values and goals? (If not, it may be time to change things up.)

Third, assess the relationships you already have. Consider the three people you currently spend the most time with: do their activities, careers, and lives reflect the goals you want to achieve? Some say that you become the average of the people with whom you spend the most time, and there's truth to that. Of course, I'm not suggesting that you should cut ties with friends or colleagues simply because some aspects of their lives or behaviors don't align with your goals, but I do believe you should make an effort to spend more time with people who do.

Productive relationships aren't transactional, but everyone enjoys a mutually beneficial relationship. In order to find people who can help you, you must find people whom you can help as well. It's not that you necessarily expect them to return the favor; instead, being a useful and generous person is a good way to build social capital. Few people forget the individuals who show up to help them in their times of need. If you provide help when it's needed, you prove yourself to be a valuable and trustworthy person.

Shrinking your inner circle gives you an opportunity to create your own environment. As you begin to move deeper into your circle, you create more authentic relationships with fewer people—just those who are truly important to you. You will gain perspective into their needs, and they, in turn, will also develop a better understanding of you. The result: a stronger platform upon which you can build a community that benefits from knowing you and your inner circle.

Determining which people will make the best fits in your network will depend on your professional goals. That's why performing a personal assessment is so important. But if you're still not sure where to start, it doesn't hurt to consider a few suggestions. Following are descriptions of character profiles that may be appropriate for your network.

The trusted confidant. As you advance through your career or undertake an entrepreneurial adventure, you may find that you need a sounding board: someone who will listen to your plans and help assess them. For this role, you want an unbiased adviser who understands the importance of discretion regarding everything you discuss. Such a person will be well rounded, well versed in a variety of topics, and able to give holistic, supportive, and constructively critical advice. Exercise caution when picking your confidant, since he or she will be the custodian of your thoughts, strategies, and fears.

The confident traveler. Someone with a good appetite for risk-taking and a highly inquisitive mind is a valuable asset for any professional network. Confident travelers are good conversationalists with immense knowledge of cultures and wide networks of people. They usually have contact information for just about everyone who crosses their path and are very resourceful. They have strong perspectives of global markets and cultures and can advise you on how and when to move out of your comfort zone. For example, if you're planning a move into an international market, he or she is the person you want to share ideas with. In fact, these folks are so confident that they might want to join you in your endeavor, since it represents an opportunity for a new adventure.

The font of inspiration. The font of inspiration is welcome in any network, no matter your goals. Why? Because even the best-laid plans will deviate off course the moment you start executing them, and you need someone who will stay with you and keep you motivated when issues arise. These off-course jaunts happen not because your plan is flawed, but rather because career plans have too many impossible-to-predict variables. This person may have direct influence on your leadership qualities, including helping to build your confidence and challenging you in ways you never thought possible. Fonts of inspiration make great mentors, as they're usually very successful in business. For that reason, always be prepared to make the most of the time spent with them, because they rarely slow down enough to let you catch up with them.

The financial genius. Money is important—very important. Whether you're working for a firm or running your business, you need people in your network who have a working knowledge of financial metrics. Such a person would have years of experience working in the finance industry or would have worked in a top-level finance position in a respectable firm. As a bonus, you can consult your financial genius about your professional finance goals or corporate investment strategies; their advice and information on organizations and businesses will be invaluable to you.

The social butterfly. Your social behavior affects your relationships and defines to whom you are attracted and who is attracted to you. In fact, in many cases, it defines the extent to which you will be able to network successfully. Usually, people who are funny and charismatic tend to have the most friends and know the most people. You probably already know someone who fits this description from school or work. Social butterflies know how to walk into a room and light it up; often, they are the life of the office party. They usually know someone who knows another someone who works somewhere. Having this kind of person in your network can help build your own charisma and confidence. Even if social butterflies don't rub shoulders with prominent people, their ability to easily form connections with people can teach you something about interacting with those who seem unapproachable. Observing them may also teach you a good bit about communication and social interactions, which you'll find useful for everything from industry events to relationships with coworkers.

No matter whom you decide to add to your inner circle, always make sure that they're truly on your side and want you to succeed. You will face challenges, and to prevail over them, you'll need a loyal team with your best interests at heart.

CHAPTER THREE

MAINTAINING YOUR INNER CIRCLE FOR THE LONG TERM

Now that you've learned about the importance of building your inner circle, it's time to cover the ins and outs of maintaining such a network over time. You'll need to know how to keep your network both strong and close, so whenever you need help, you can easily reach out. It's also important to know how frequently you should keep in touch with your inner circle, as well as the intricacies of bringing new people into the fold while still maintaining communication with those you've known for a while. If you fail to stay in close touch with your inner circle, you'll miss out on a lot of opportunities.

A key part of maintaining your inner circle is determining which members get priority. It's often helpful to categorize your network. For example, you can group your network into current clients, powerful colleagues, friends who are high connectors, and so on. Then, based on your needs and goals, decide how you want to allocate your attention. It's best to think carefully about how the relationships you have with your inner circle affect you: do you feel happy after ending a phone conversation with him or her? Do they help you find solutions to your problems? If you find that time and again, you're either happier or closer to your goal after talking or meeting with a particular person, you should prioritize that relationship accordingly. Some people may be in your inner circle simply because you enjoy their company, and that's okay.

The world is now a global village. Wherever you are, communication tools allow you to keep in touch with everyone. You can reach out using email or social media apps, or simply make a phone call. For a more personal touch, request a coffee date or send a handwritten note. What tools you deploy to nurture your relationships are up to you, but the key to maintaining your inner circle is to stay within what I call your circle's "mental vision." Your contact doesn't necessarily have to be physical, but it needs to keep you top of mind.

An effective way to accomplish this is through acts showing that you care about the person and remain interested in them. For example, when news or other information triggers you to think of a person, let him or her know about it. Perhaps you discovered something you know the person has always wanted, or you discussed a favorite topic with someone else. Or maybe you met a mutual connection and exchanged memories about him or her. All of these are great opportunities to reach out. Don't restrict your contact with members of your inner circle to moments when you're in need. Good relationships require nurturing in order to blossom.

It also helps to use social media strategically. The apps that connect us all allow us to easily stay linked to people for as long as they live—but there is a caveat. Over-reliance on social media as a way of maintaining relationships with your inner circle can complicate matters. In much the same way a face-to-face meeting almost always beats a phone call, social media has a different level of fidelity. We often feel like we have strong connections with people on those platforms, despite the fact that sometimes, our relationships with them never leave those platforms.

Notwithstanding, you *should* use social media to your advantage. Send your inner circle direct messages or share their posts on Facebook or LinkedIn. Retweet their articles or thought-leadership tweets on Twitter. Just remember: it's always better to take conversations offline. For example, if you learn of a connection's promotion or job change on LinkedIn, it pays to send a handwritten note or a card with a congratulatory message or call to offer your best wishes much more warmly. Make it personal and go out of your way to offer your support and congratulations.

Be Helpful

The whole point of having inner circles is for all participants to benefit from them. One of the best ways to sustain a good relationship is by looking for opportunities to help your connections. Listen very carefully to their challenges and help them sort things out, if you can. If one of your important connections has a niece or sibling looking for an internship, for example, you can reach out to your own manager or others in your professional or personal networks to see if they know of any opportunities. Perhaps you have a coworker who is planning an event and needs some help; offer your assistance in some way—maybe you could loan a grill, or a truck, or anything else that might be needed.

When you're offering help, always be sure your motive is clear. It's always good to help others, but if you're doing so only to gain favor at some later date, your avarice will be transparent. You'll show them that you're looking out for yourself or that you just want to impress—

and no one appreciates that. Hiding your true intentions is a fast route to losing the respect of people who are important to you.

Be Humble

While it's good for people in your network to know about your professional success, you must be careful about the way you communicate about it. You don't want to appear to be a braggart. Simply keep your inner circle informed about what you've been up to and share news about how you can be helpful to them thanks to your success. Avoid making it seem like a promotional campaign—just share your successes. And if members of your inner circle played a role in that success, be sure to acknowledge as much.

Be Respectful

You can't force these relationships. If you've tried multiple times to keep in touch with someone and he or she doesn't seem to be interested in staying connected, it's probably best to let it be. Don't burden yourself with the stresses of a relationship that isn't mutual; just as with any relationship, you should get as much out of it as you put into it. Don't force a connection if one isn't there.

Be Thankful

Keep track of all that others have done for you. The people in your inner circle deserve recognition and appreciation. You didn't get to where you are today alone. Take a moment to pause and flash back on the life-changing decisions you've made that got you to this place in your career. More than a few of them probably came about thanks to advice someone gave you or something another person said that made you think twice about the path you were on. At some point, each and every one of us have shared the same experience: a family member, coworker, boss, mentor, teammate, friend, or other significant figure in our life has put us on a certain path to help us achieve satisfaction in our life or career. For example:

- Someone who encouraged you to apply for a job you didn't think you were qualified for.
- A friend who offered support while you struggled to find a job that inspired you.
- A mentor who recommended that you change your career path to a more rewarding option.
- Team members who took the time to review your projects and proposals numerous times and offered feedback on them before you turned them in or presented them.
- A significant other who was always there to help you decompress after a long day at work and who keeps encouraging you, even on days when you're at your wits' end.
- A friend who reviewed your resume and helped you prepare for a final interview.

If you're capable of introspection, you'll find that you won't be able to thank these people enough. In reality, there are far too many people in your professional history to thank, but if you practice appreciation one person at a time, you'll be on the right track.

Be Mindful

Many of us are quick to gloss over the relationships we have with people who were there for us when we first got a new job or had some other significant development in our careers. We suddenly become too busy to make time for those who took the time to lend their support when we needed it. Perhaps this neglect takes the form of failing to respond to calls, emails, or texts as fast as we should. Over time, this neglect will likely lead us to lose contact with them completely, or (worse yet) we may end up only reaching out when we need something from them. Take some time today—right now—to reach out and thank people who fit this description. Connect to them in a real, genuine, and grateful way.

Never forget those who helped you get where you are today. In my experience, many people close to me, both personally and professionally, have helped shape my career and my reputation as a leader. Sometimes, even the smallest bits of advice I've received—which I may or may not have recognized as the important wisdom they were at the time—have had the longest-lasting impact. Recognize and acknowledge the people who have helped you, and make sure to keep them in your inner circle. Repaying a debt is a good feeling.

CHAPTER FOUR

NETWORKING RIGHT

I don't know about you, but when I stand in the checkout line at Walmart, or Target, or the grocery store, I usually take a quick (and discreet) peek at the gossip magazines that have been strategically placed at the checkout counter. Fortunately, you don't have to look long, as the covers blare out the half-truths of celebrities' lives. If I'm not doing that, I'm eyeing all the attractively wrapped candy while trying to have a casual conversation with the checkout clerk or another customer in the line. "What do you think about this brand?" "I always pick the slowest line." "Oh! What aisle did you get that from?"

We all like to chat—even introverts. Sometimes, conversations can be so fun and engaging that you end up disclosing a lot of personal information and sometimes even exchange contact information. Casual chit-chat happens everywhere: on planes, at grocery stores, at the park, in restaurants. We make connections all the time, no matter how brief they may be, and sometimes these connections grow and blossom into lifelong friendships. After all, this is likely how you met the people whom you consider to be your closest friends.

Networking is about making connections, building and developing relationships, and creating opportunities in your professional life. It's also a strategy to create lasting connections and relationships in every aspect of your life. People come into your world for different reasons and durations, and if you ruminate on it a bit, you might find that some of the people currently in your life are there to satisfy a need that you may have expressed, whether the expression was deliberate or subconscious. They may be there to provide some form of physical, emotional, spiritual, or professional support—without you even realizing it.

Be Positive

When trying to build relationships, one of the best strategies is to remain positive and enthusiastic. The best networkers know how to attract people; they're the ones you enjoy spending time with. People with strong networks tend to be positive, upbeat, and enthusiastic about the future and what it holds. Positivity and enthusiasm are essential to growing your social capital. No one wants to spend time with people who focus on the negative, are often critical, or have low self-esteem. Such negativity drains away energy and emotions. Wouldn't you prefer to spend time with someone who makes you feel good about yourself and the future?

Be Willing to Try New Things

You've probably heard the saying, "The only thing that is certain in life is change." Businesses flourish or fail. People change and move on, and their careers change, too. Your inner circle may change as well. What's key is to know how these changes affect you and when to change your network. There will always be opportunities to network, but the question is, are you ready to take the leap? A willingness to experiment and connect can help direct you and help you figure out how to best allocate your time in order to maximize the return for your effort.

Curiosity and a desire to try new things are two sides of the same coin. The best networkers are people who are curious by nature; they're curious about people, professions, new experiences, and businesses. This curiosity helps them find common ground and rapport with the people they meet.

Be Tenacious and Persistent

A common career mistake is to wait to invest effort in building and maintaining your network until just around the time you need it—say, the beginning of a job hunt. Frantically reaching out to people you haven't connected with in several months (or years) in hopes of getting information about a job opportunity or some other information—it doesn't really sound like a recipe for success, does it?

A strong network requires staying in touch, even when doing so feels inconvenient. Never wait until you need something to reach out to the people in your network. Think of your network as a tree—you must first plant a seed, and then water it routinely in order to get it to bear fruit. It may not bear fruit for the first six months, or even for years. But if you continue to water it and care for it, someday, the fruit will bloom. If you plan to enjoy the fruits of your labor before the tree ever has a chance to flourish, you'll likely be disappointed.

In the end, if you nurture your network and have patience, tenacity, and persistence, the referrals, opportunities, and recommendations you long for will come.

Be Courageous

Many people are afraid to send emails or LinkedIn requests to people who have a high profile in their industry. Such fear can often stand in the way of progress and opportunities. If this description fits you, you may be grafting misconceptions you have about social etiquette and these people in leadership positions based on the current positions they occupy, the authority they might have, and the experience they possess. You'd be surprised: many high-profile people and industry experts are willing to have a productive conversation with pretty much anyone who's ready to listen.

If you're afraid to talk to someone because of his or her position, experience, or popularity, pause to take a breath and remind yourself that your target's a human being, just like you, regardless of any accomplishments or titles. Tear down the imaginary barrier and the self-limiting beliefs you've constructed, because they're standing in the way of your networking strategy. If you seek a highly influential mentor, just ask, but be sure to explain why you chose that person. Plenty of people will be flattered and will end up saying yes.

Be a good networker. See the person and not the title. Be brave enough to start a conversation that just might make a huge difference in your career and business.

Be Grateful

Many times, it's not who you know—it's who you *appreciate*. We're taught from a very young age about the importance of appreciation, including always saying "thank you." Once you're all grown up, it's just as important as it was when you were a child. *Always* thank the people with whom you share business and personal relationships. Expressing your appreciation to clients, coworkers, employees, and friends makes a serious difference in their attitudes toward you, and positive attitudes directly affect business and personal success.

One effective method to thank a connection is to give a gift. Gifts aren't just an expression of gratitude—they're also a reminder of you, tokens that keep you in the recipient's thoughts. After meetings, seminars, or presentations, I often stay in touch with the people I connect with by sending a small gift either right after the connection is made or by following up at least once every three months with small tokens of appreciation—just something to keep my name visible. During the holidays, I send my important connections thank-you gifts with my name and a personal message attached.

For an extra layer of personal touch, find gifts that fit your recipients' specific interests. Always consider what will be appreciated the most.

Depth Matters

The relative depth of your personal relationships, both inside and outside work, is a very important consideration. While time is a major constraint and often stands in the way of forming deep connections with the people in our network, you must make it a priority.

Forming deep relationships with a few people is, of course, much easier than trying to do so with everyone in your network. These strong, trust-based relationships just might translate to wider access to professional opportunities. To figure out which members of your network you should form deep relationships with, the single most critical factor to consider is their willingness to recommend you. If they're not... well, maybe it's best not to focus too much attention and effort on those relationships.

Many professionals and students want to network, but they fear they lack the skills to do it effectively. Networking tools are abundant: LinkedIn, Facebook, Twitter, Meetup... the list seems endless. Networking tools often try to leave users with the impression that connections on their platforms will always blossom into valuable relationships. But networking is not as easy as it seems, and there's no app that can make it magically happen for you.

Social media platforms are powerful tools that shouldn't be underestimated, but the truth is that deep connections aren't formed there. In real life, networking is even more challenging and complex than it's ever been. Now, there are so many more relationships to manage, perspectives to consider, emails to respond to, and items on our to-do lists to complete. Your growing list of contacts alone can create an aversion to networking. For this reason, truly effective, high-value, and high-quality networking requires connecting with people beyond the fringes of social media. To do it, you've got to cut through the clutter and focus on what truly matters—relationships that are real, mutual, and beneficial.

The average person has around 150 people in his or her network. That's a lot of people, so closely examine the ones in yours and decide which are the best candidates for deeper relationships. Then, get busy becoming closer to and better acquainted with them. Networking is about opening and developing opportunities by getting out there and meeting people and then connecting the dots (i.e., strengthening those relationships) where and when necessary. Start building your inner circle now by taking a hard look at your current network of:

Customers and clients. Depending on your industry, your customers and clients can be your brand evangelists, including spreading the word about your best qualities and providing you with strong, honest, and useful feedback. Look for opportunities to be a reference for them, help them, and keep in touch.

Colleagues and coworkers. The people you spend most of your time with on a daily basis can be powerful resources for networking. Invite a coworker to join you for a weekend activity or event. Get to know him or her better; building alliances within your company is an effective way to gradually build success.

Fellow alumni and former classmates. Never miss an opportunity to reconnect with people from your past. Keeping in touch with former classmates is a good way to stay up to date on their careers and get information about the companies where they work, job opportunities, and potential business partnerships that may be very beneficial to you in the long run. You may find that some are like-minded; grow your relationships with them and use activities and events as ways to intensify your bonds.

Neighbors. Put yourself out there and get to know the people who live near you. Turn a quick hello into a conversation and open the door to a new relationship.

Friends and family. Your family and friends are in your life already; take the time to nurture and strengthen those bonds. Your emotional health is dependent on having good relationships with them. Network with friends and family in a positive way, but avoid the temptation to exploit those relationships or have unrealistic expectations of what they will yield. Think about what you can to do to help support their goals or aid them in a time of need.

Random people. Keep your eyes and your mind open for any and all possibilities. You can learn more every day if you pay attention to what goes on around you. As time goes by, and as you build trust and rapport, these associations can lead to other possibilities, a wider range of contacts, and more valuable relationships.

CHAPTER FIVE

NETWORKING TO GET JOBS

Countless articles and books have been written about how to land the job you want. Most of these works focus on the front end of the process: searching for jobs using job sites, filling out applications, writing good cover letters, preparing for interviews, and negotiating a salary. Don't get me wrong: all of these are important elements, but when it comes to advancing your career and reaching the next level, this standard process falls short.

For these types of roles, the true game changers in your career, the path must run through your network. Your inner circle shouldn't just be a list of people you know—instead, it's the people who will help open doors when the time is right, who will stake their own reputations to recommend you to others. And the only way to have a connection like this is to create deeper relationships that go well beyond what can be gleaned from a résumé.

One of the advantages of having an inner circle is the access they provide to job opening announcements before they become public, as well as insider tips on what hiring managers are seeking in the ideal candidate. If you have built a strong network, this will come very naturally to you, and you'll always be in the know about such opportunities. Of course, a network this strong will take some time and effort, but the payoff is undeniable.

Imagine finding the job of your dreams—and then discovering that a member of your inner circle is on the committee that will make the hiring decision. More often than not, it's a game changer. The effort you've invested in articulating the values you share with your connection at the firm could make all the difference. While a robust network may help any career grow, positions in senior leadership, like C-level roles, are much more likely to be filled by word of mouth. Your network of close, trusted colleagues and peers will become your door openers, recommending you to anyone who will listen. They will speak well of you and help build your brand, even when you're not around.

That said, never fall into the trap of thinking, "Since I know someone at the company, I'll definitely get this job." That's a fundamentally unrealistic mindset, as things rarely play out that way in the end. At times in my career, a door has been opened for me by the relationships I have created; but remember that other people are opening those same doors for their connections as well. Nothing is guaranteed, so avoid making the assumption that it is.

No matter who you might know, you're not always going to get the job. Never place blame; instead, be appreciative of the opportunity that was offered to you and ask for feedback. It's a rare opportunity to see if there might be something you could have done differently to improve your chances of success. Learn from these moments and you will help your career grow, even if you didn't get the job.

Handling Job Ads

Now that I've touched on the importance of approaching a job search with the right mindset, it's time to talk about how to actually land a job. If you've been busy connecting with people, building your network, and showcasing your skills and experience, good news: you've done about 90 percent of the work. The remaining 10 percent involves navigating through job postings and requirements to find what you are looking for.

Once you start to sift through job postings, you'll likely find that most seek applicants whose skills or experience are not a direct match with yours—don't let that scare you off. One of the greatest advantages of your network is its ability to help you to translate the buzzwords of a multitude of industry languages. Reach out to someone in your network within the industry and ask for help in decoding the posting.

The secret to getting a job in a field that differs from most of your background isn't just an ability to use industry buzzwords—it's an ability to articulate your understanding and viewpoints in plain, simple language. Deep dives with members of your network will give you a new breadth of understanding of the field, and you'll be ready when it's time to find a posting that fits your aspirations.

Let's take this a step further: when the time comes for you to begin applying for jobs, don't hesitate to apply to jobs for which you meet some, but not all, of the criteria. Keep the focus singular: only apply for jobs you really want and in which you are confident you can succeed. If the role (and the company) are a good match for your career goals, don't let the job's predetermined criteria stand in your way.

The application process is an energy- and time-consuming process; therefore, you need to set your priorities. A strong network makes this process much easier to figure out. Your best tactic is to try to get jobs at organizations where people you know work. Finding out about those opportunities early on is key. Many people choose to press their connections for information. For example, if a friend of yours works at an organization where you've seen an appealing opportunity, you might ask him or her out to lunch and ask questions like:

- Do you have any helpful tips about job opportunities within the organization?
- How do you recommend I approach the hiring manager?
- Any tips on how I can secure the job?
- Do you think I should apply for this job?
- What are the politics like there?
- What should I feature on my résumé to get noticed?
- Is this job really open as it's advertised?

But remember: your friend has only one perspective. He or she might be harboring negative sentiments or grievances—or maybe just isn't all that perceptive. In the end, you must follow your own best judgment and know what to act upon and believe. There are many other ways to learn the details about open jobs. For example, others around have their own networks, too, and can find out and pass along useful information.

Maximizing Networking Opportunities

An excellent way to grow your inner circle and become more adept at socializing professionally—especially if you're focused on a certain industry—is to attend industry events, such as trade shows, conferences, and seminars. Industry events provide opportunities to meet people at all levels within a particular industry in a more relaxed environment that fosters conversations, mentorships, collaborations, and relationships (they're also a great way to learn enough about the industry to become conversant and maybe even to feel comfortable enough to initiate conversations about hot industry topics). At industry events, you'll have an opportunity to meet people you may not normally have easy access to, such as C-suite level executives and managers.

Industry events open the door to a lot of opportunities. In 2010, I spoke at a local industry event of digital marketing professionals, and within only a few hours, I'd gathered an impressive stack of business cards and plenty of connection requests on LinkedIn. While I haven't spoken with many of the people I met that day since, a few have become business associates and valued resources for my own career advancement.

Your first step in maximizing the opportunities industry events can offer is to get comfortable with talking to total strangers. Put yourself out there, and get comfortable with small talk. In truth, most valuable conversations start with seemingly inconsequential chit-chat. For example, a quick conversation with a sales rep about a company-branded shirt she's wearing could lead to insider scoop about the organization's culture and what it's planning to do next. So, to make the most of a networking event, master the art of the quick and easy conversation. If you're an introvert—as many of us are—and this is difficult for you, the next paragraph should provide help.

If needed, you can mentally prepare a list of ice breakers to help you ease into conversations. What are ice breakers? Well, they're conversation starters you can use to engage your person of interest, and they also serve to sustain the conversation because you can come up with questions based on their responses. For example, you can get things started with questions like:

- "Have you been to one of these meetings before?"
- "Which session did you enjoy the most?"
- "Whom have you enjoyed meeting so far?

From their responses to your questions, you can find common ground.

Your goal should be to find people with whom you share similar interests or backgrounds and see if it's possible to grow relationships with them in the future. Sometimes, things won't turn out the way you hope. Conversations may become boring. One party might end up talking too much. Another might not talk enough. Just stay focused on the main idea: put some effort into it, and stay interested in learning more about the person behind the name tag.

Of course, it always helps to have a backup plan, just in case. If what I've described sounds too difficult, ask a friend in the industry to come with you. He or she might be able to introduce you to two or three people they know; you might find that a lot easier than engaging in conversations with total strangers.

CHAPTER SIX

WORKING WITH PEOPLE

You may or may not initially agree with this statement, but deep down… you really do care what other people think of you. You care about being liked. You care about whether people think you are smart, competent, or skilled. When you're working in a group, you want to be accepted. You want people to agree with you and to talk with you. A fundamental desire for social acceptance is part of being human, and striving for this acceptance is critical to developing good relationships and building valuable networks.

Many of us make the mistake of thinking that overachieving and being intelligent, smart, and competent are all the characteristics we need to make progress in the workplace. Of course, it's very important to have those qualities—especially when you're in an entry-level role—but in order to be able to lead teams, achieve goals, and get people to do your bidding, you're going to need more.

Specifically, you need to be likeable. Being smart and competent will get you respect, but likeability gets people to rally around you as a leader. How you're perceived by the people you work with, from supervisors to coworkers, can to an extent determine the rate at which you will ascend up the corporate ladder. Always be on the lookout for ways to make others want to work with you, because that is the most important element of success. If you take the time to encourage trust among your peers and colleagues, showcase your expertise, build a culture for success, and prove that you're worthy of their loyalty, people will want to work with you—or for you.

Make Others Want to Be Around You

Your life as a leader will be much easier if the people who work for you already like you, respect you, and believe in your vision. You probably already know the basics of how to foster this type of positive work environment: don't talk behind other people's backs, be considerate, be decent, and so on. But there are quite a few more techniques you can employ to make people want to work with you.

Use names. In some ways, we're all narcissistic. We like to feel important and love to hear our names spoken. It's always good practice in business to make a point of remembering names, and it's best if you remember after being told only once. When you remember a new acquaintance's name, it makes the person feel that he or she must matter to you.

When conversing with others, especially when you meet someone new—perhaps at an industry event—be sure to use their names in conversation. "So, Dale, what are your thoughts about object-oriented programming?" is far better than "What are your thoughts about object-oriented programming?" Names are more than what they appear to be: using them shows that you are paying attention and can be very effective in disarming people, especially in situations where they don't expect you to remember.

Smile. It seems simple, right? Making a point to smile more often can help soften others' perspectives towards you. Smiling is a feedback tool that shows social cooperation. Your smile could brighten someone's day or make them more receptive to your request. In most cases, you can't go wrong when you smile while working with people. Your visibly positive attitude just might make another person's day better and he or she will appreciate you for that and will be more willing to talk to and work with you.

Listen actively. Everyone likes a good listener, someone who can listen without needing to interrupt and offer one's own opinion or perspective. Give people the attention they need—and that starts with giving them your full attention. A good start is to put away your cell phone when someone is talking to you—even if the person is a longtime friend. Face the other person and mirror his or her stance. Maintain eye contact and give frequent nonverbal cues that you are hearing the person loud and clear. You can also show you are listening actively by repeating a part of what your conversation partner says. Here's an example:

Laura: The team from the client really loved our media presentation, and as a next step, they want to dive into the specific costs of the proposal.

You: Oh, I'm so glad they liked the presentation. Well done! Can you share with me which of the specific costs in the proposal they wish to discuss?

Acknowledging what the other person says and seeking additional clarification is a very effective way to show a conversation partner that you're really listening. When you echo back parts of the conversation, the other person feels important and you show that you are paying attention. It feels good to know that others appreciate our words.

Recalling past conversations is another effective strategy to show people that their conversations with you count and matter. For example, you might ask a coworker, "Matt, how did your son's baseball game go last week?" This question clearly recalls a prior conversation. Even if a conversation is on a personal level, showing how well you listened and remembered it can have long-lasting impact.

Give feedback. Everyone loves to be appreciated and to receive authentic praise. That's not to be confused with empty flattery, which many people can easily detect. People want to be genuinely appreciated for their effort. If people on your team do something right, let them know about it. Don't withhold genuine appreciation. When it's clear that you mean what you say to a friend or colleague, you encourage a sense of trust. The other person will know not only that you care, but also that you wish him or her to be recognized for contributions to the team.

It's just as important to provide feedback when there are opportunities for improvement. Delivering constructive feedback is a challenge, but when done properly, it improves a relationship. Feedback isn't intended as criticism; instead, it's designed to help others improve, which will benefit them as well as their careers. If it's delivered well, feedback of this sort will be valued even more than compliments or recognition.

Avoid giving orders. Unless you're in the military, where giving orders is a way of life, avoid the practice. No one likes to be bossed around. If you need something done, just ask nicely—you'll get the same result without the resentment that often follows being ordered about. Instead of saying, "Tate, I need you to send that report ASAP," say, "Hi, Tate, can you send that report as soon as you can? I'd really appreciate it if you could make it a top priority." The second statement essentially says the same thing but empowers Tate to strive to meet your expectations, instead of a demand.

Be yourself. People like to see the real, authentic you. Many things are better left for life outside of work, but you must also be true to yourself while surrounded by your coworkers and colleagues. You are trying to build relationships, and that becomes so much harder if you're pretending to be someone other than yourself. Remember the one constant that got you to where you are now: you.

Ask for advice. Seeking advice is a surprisingly effective strategy to encourage others to respect and appreciate you. Doing so shows that you value the other person's opinion, and people like to be wanted and valued. Asking for their opinion or advice communicates that you value them, and also that you're comfortable with asking for help. Demonstrating some degree of vulnerability—meaning indicating that you don't know everything and are okay with looking to others for help—is an important trait in a leader. If you believe that two heads are better than one, three heads are better than two, and so on, you'll understand why asking for help or advice can work well to improve a team.

Asking Questions

It also pays to ask questions. When you work with others, it's often easier to form bonds and strengthen your relationship if you ask them questions about their lives, interests, passions, and activities outside of work. Most of us have an egocentric side, so if you give others the opportunity to talk about themselves and show genuine interest in their responses, they'll leave the conversation thinking highly of you. Even people who don't often speak about themselves appreciate it when an attempt is made to learn more about them and to think of them as more than just another coworker.

Don't forget: your goal is to develop genuine relationships with your coworkers. In reality, you may not be able to do this with each and every person you work with, but you should always strive to do it at least with the people in your immediate environment. Your goal should not be to make relationships simply for the sake of having them—in other words, you shouldn't be reaching out solely because you need them to like you in order to benefit your career. Certainly, that's one of the advantages of having good working relationships, but the moment you take on that mindset, you undermine the possibility of forming genuine relationships.

Befriending someone because you need something from them isn't relationship building—it's a transaction. Instead, approach others with a sense of curiosity. Make an effort to genuinely care about them, their roles, and their lives outside of the workplace. In other words, try to develop empathy.

Now, if your job is little more than tolerable and is nothing more to you than a source of income, this may be difficult for you. It'll be even more difficult if you've previously benefited from, or are still benefiting from, transactional relationships. But the truth is that transactional relationships aren't the best way to build a network. They won't deliver the trusted inner circle you need to succeed. Most painful of all is the realization that people with whom you have these types of relationships won't think of you when an opportunity comes along, because you were never in their hearts. The moment you're out of sight, they no longer find you useful.

A good way to start is by finding something that piques your curiosity about people in your immediate environment and talk to them about it, all while being mindful of the tactics above. Making people like you, and building genuine relationships with them, is made much easier by initiating and sustaining meaningful conversations.

Getting Noticed

Most of us know people who seem to be "go-to people" for just about anything. They're the first people you consider whenever you have an issue that needs fixing—anything from broken computers to broken relationships. If there's a whisper in the office about upcoming pay raises, bonuses, or layoffs, they're usually the first to know. If something seems totally impossible to get done, they're the ones who are called on to make it happen. Other people find them valuable, and they always get noticed.

Most of the time, these people excel at what they do. Everyone wants to interact with and delegate high-stakes tasks to subordinates who know what they're doing and who don't disappoint. High-stakes projects are usually in the limelight, so getting the opportunity to work on them (and succeed) is also an opportunity for you to shine and get more recognition. This brings us to the next point.

People always want to talk to useful people. If you want to make it easy for others to work with you, don't pass up an opportunity to make a genuine offer to help. Don't wait for them to ask. If a coworker is in distress and you make an offer to help despite the fact that he or she hasn't even asked for your help, you're likely to be appreciated and remembered by that person—much more so than if your help had been requested.

It also helps to volunteer for projects or assignments when you can; it's another chance to show management and coworkers how great you are. But be sure not to be too self-promoting in the process. Volunteer because you want to lend your expertise to a project, and not because you want all eyes on you.

Handling Feedback and Criticism

As mentioned earlier, feedback is an important part of any relationship, whether it's in the workplace or in your personal life. Feedback is necessary for growth and improvement. It can be positive or negative, of course, and it's the negative feedback that many people can't handle well. For many, the moment the words start rolling out, their heartbeat accelerates, and they immediately become defensive, trying to figure out ways to rationalize whatever actions might have led to the criticism. And usually, in the heat of the moment, tensions rise and anger may be a consequence. Before anyone can say anything else, the relationship may become strained.

Handling criticism requires skill and practice. It requires being deliberate about making changes and being willing to put in the work to make those changes happen. Figuring out how to effectively receive feedback was an issue for me in the early stages of my career. I'd hear the feedback as a personal attack, rather than an effort to help me improve. Once I learned to take a step back and ask questions designed to help me understand the core meaning of the feedback, I was able to appreciate what others had to say. If you find yourself on the receiving end of feedback, take a deep breath and ask yourself, "What is this person really trying to say? What suggestions to help me improve can I find within the message?"

By taking a calm approach, you can avoid one of the pitfalls of receiving feedback: saying something you might regret. Many of us find silence uncomfortable, so we often try to fill it—and sometimes that results in saying something you'll wish you hadn't. Try to resist the urge. Becoming comfortable with silences in conversations enables you to think deeply about what's been said and to come up with a measured response.

Hear people out. Just listen. Avoid cutting in, chipping in your opinion, or responding midway into the speech. By letting people totally express themselves and listening to what they have to say, without immediately thinking about how to respond, you'll be in a much better position to make sense of what they're saying. Once you're both able to agree that something needs work, it's up to you to go ahead and fix it.

If the problem you're dealing with is behavioral, then it may require some degree of tact to effect change. The best way to deal with bad habits is to replace them completely. When trying to break bad habits, many rely on the power of commitment and willpower alone. But willpower is limited, and if you're physically, emotionally, or cognitively spent, the effort is even greater.

You have to know the triggers for your bad habits. What triggers your tendency to speak rudely to people? What makes you stay in bed instead of getting up and starting your day? Many people who have successfully overcome alcoholism have found that staying away from family and friends who drink helps them fight the disease—no more nights socializing in bars, and no more beer kept in the fridge for visitors. Alcoholics who suffer from depression are often advised to spend more time with the people and things that make them happy, so they don't have to resort to alcohol to deliver temporary happiness.

These strategies are based on removing triggers. If you tend to snap at people when you're exhausted, for example, you need to make sure you don't mix with colleagues when you're overly tired. If you've been told that you tend to react impulsively, and you work in an environment where you frequently interact with your coworkers, it's wise to set a rule for yourself that you'll take a ten-second pause before you react to a burning issue. Simply count in your head from one to ten; by the time you've finished counting, you've given yourself more time to develop a better response or reaction to the issue. If you work to become more conscious of your impulses and practice the countdown technique before reacting, in no time at all, your impulsive behavior will reduce substantially. When you embark on changing your habits, you should first consider your long-term goals, but then take a short-term focus on making changes. In the above example of changing impulsive behavior, you effect the change by becoming more conscious of your reactions slowly, on a daily basis.

Getting rid of a bad habit is also easier when you have an accountability partner. Share the whole truth with your partner: tell him or her why you want to change the habit, what triggers it, and how the person can help you. And when you slip up, turn to your accountability partner for support and guidance. Partners can help you stay strong in future situations.

Be open to feedback from within your circle, as well as from people outside of it. Sometimes those who are the closest to you are in the best position to give you advice on personal and professional matters; at other times, those who don't know you well but who understand your ideas may be the best people to weigh in. This is why it's so vital to have trust-based relationships.

Communicating Ideas

Anyone who's into digital marketing has probably heard of Seth Godin, a well-known author and entrepreneur. Godin has achieved phenomenal success in the marketing field, and when I listened to a podcast interview of Godin by Krista Tippett, I noticed a pattern: throughout the session, whenever Tippett asked Godin about his views on a particular topic, he would start his response with an interesting story or an experience that was sure to get you hooked. Godin concluded each of these topics by drawing points from the story—points that were tough to disagree with. Telling stories is Godin's style, and it's made him very successful at convincing people to buy things they don't really need.

Now, you may not be in the business of making people buy things they don't need, but either consciously or subconsciously, we're all in the business of making people love our ideas. Whether your objective is to convince your boss that a get-together will be great for department morale, or to make your spouse understand why your family should visit your parents this weekend, being able to convince people to love your ideas is a skill everyone should seek to improve—especially in the workplace.

When it comes to marketing for e-consumers, Godin is probably the master. He knows his stuff. And if you want to make people love your idea, you need to know your stuff, too, inside and out. It's not enough to have jolts of inspiration and to gush on and on about it. You've got to think your ideas through and through, weighing the pros against the cons, coming up with every possible question that might come up, and being ready with well-thought-out answers to those questions.

If you have an upcoming presentation, it's considered good practice to share your idea with a friend first. If, after explaining the idea to your friend, he or she is still staring at you like a deer in headlights, you know you still have work to do.

Part of getting others to love your ideas is caring enough to get to know their tendencies—that is, how they are likely to react—and planning accordingly. If, for example, your boss is a direct and borderline-aggressive person, you should learn to cut to the chase when convincing him about an idea. Don't waste his time talking about prologues that don't really matter. But if your boss likes details and analysis, be sure to have at the ready some stats, case studies, arguments, analysis, and so on that will make them love your idea and help convince them they should do things your way.

Now, let's assume that they do love your idea. Does that mean it will come to fruition right away? Probably not. As part of making people love your ideas, you must also remove all barriers to the execution of such ideas. This may involve quite a bit of pre-planning and anticipation of concerns. Sometimes even trying to coordinate schedules to meet with the team can be challenge, so moving the project forward may require reshuffling of priorities by multiple people.

Some say that ideas rule the world; but making it easy for people to work with you to execute ideas is what really rocks. Once you've removed the barriers, you need to gain support. Remember when you were a kid and you wanted to get your dad to do something he wouldn't ordinarily do? Your first move would likely be to ask your mom or siblings first, so they could back you up.

That's family politics; but a modified version of it works in the boardroom, too. If you're presenting a wild idea and need the powers that be to love it so much that they're willing to put their signatures to it, it's always good to first check out your idea with your colleagues or supervisors to see if they will back you up. Plan ahead, so you don't have to walk alone.

Handling Rumors

Most offices have a rumor mill. It's distracting, yet also inevitable. It is human nature to gossip, and depending on how information is typically handled in your organization, rumors may or may not gain a foothold. Rumors are most common in large organizations, where the chain of command is long and staff are rarely updated about happenings. Chances are that you've taken part in circulating rumors, either by providing an ear or actively sharing one.

When rumors relate to the underlying business, such as those about an acquisition or layoffs, leaders must get out in front of these conversations before they have a chance to completely disrupt the flow of work. In a 2012 *Forbes* article, Holly Green wrote, "When you communicate with people consistently and frequently, they won't depend on the grapevine (of rumors). But if you leave them in the dark on important information, and individuals believe they can obtain fairly reliable sources elsewhere, your grapevine will inevitably grow." Great advice, indeed.

CHAPTER SEVEN

LEADING RIGHT

L eadership authority John Maxwell once said, "Leadership is influence. Nothing more, nothing less." But let's broaden the definition of leadership a little bit more.

Leadership can be described as the relationship between a person (the leader) and a group of people (the followers or team members) in which the person uses his or her skills and intellectual capacity to successfully guide the group toward a common goal. Take note of the words used in this description: relationship, skills, intellectual capacity, guide, group, common goal. All of these words make a lot of difference in leadership.

For instance, a leader may perform exceptionally well in one group and underperform in another for many reasons. For one, underperformance can result if a group does not sense that it is a part of the leader's trusted team, which happens when the leader lacks the skill to carry the group along in the achievement of the goal. A leader inspires his or her team to join together and achieve a common goal and shared success. In every corner of the world, good leadership is what every group yearns for, what every association, union, and citizen of every nation clamors for, because good leadership touches lives and positively changes them forever.

I've had the opportunity to speak about leadership on many occasions. I've discussed and interacted with everyone from business leaders and entrepreneurs to corporate executives and blue-collar workers. I've found that people choose to follow leaders who inspire and motivate them. They follow leaders with whom they feel a connection, both professionally and personally.

Building your skills as a leader is perhaps one of the most important factors in growing your professional career. As part of this up-leveling, you'll learn techniques that will help set the foundation for your role as a leader.

Build Trust

Good leadership is emotional. People feel attached to those they trust. Nobody wants to spend time with a person who talks tough, yet acts feebly, or someone whose words and actions can't be trusted—especially if this person is in a leadership position. People expect you to say something and then act on it. Leading involves getting the people around you to trust your words, and more importantly, to trust that you will come through on your promises. But trust takes time. It doesn't just happen overnight. It is slowly earned and is built on a platform of honesty and integrity. When people work with you, they want to trust you to safeguard their interests. They want to go to bed each night knowing that your protection over them is undeniable.

As we have seen throughout history, especially in political or financial services circles, lies and cover-ups anger the population more than deceptive acts themselves. Look no further than the Watergate scandal of the 1970s, or even a few years ago, when Volkswagen revealed that it had installed software on millions of diesel-powered cars and SUVs in order to trick the Environmental Protection Agency's emission testers into thinking that the cars were more eco-friendly than they were. Understandably, investors and consumers deserted the company. Why? It's a matter of trust. If I'm going to trust you with my support or my money, then I must be completely sure that you have my best interests at heart. Once that trust is broken, getting it back is an uphill battle with no clear resolution.

The same is true for managers in the workplace. No one likes a leader who promises a bonus and then ends up telling you how it won't be possible. It is important that people can take your word to the bank, both figuratively and literally. If you say you're going to come through, ensure that you keep your promise. It's endemic to the human condition that sometimes, circumstances may keep you from fulfilling a promise. That's why you should only make commitments when they are very likely to occur.

Much as your parents likely taught you as a child, telling the truth is always the best solution, and the same is true when you're in positions of leadership. In many cases, people will forgive you quickly for a transgression if you tell them the truth; but that forgiveness is much less likely if you try hard to cover it up and they uncover those lies themselves. Even if you don't currently occupy a leadership position, you never know who's watching and observing you.

The moment you start working in a new place, you have the potential to become a leader there. Many CEOs and company executives started as entry-level employees at some point in their careers. Not everyone starts their own company or inherits one from their parents—in fact, a small minority rises to the top in this way. Very small. Even if you do belong to this small minority, you still need to have a good working relationship with your colleagues in order to achieve success in your role. For this, trust is key.

Lead with Integrity

If you promise paradise to everyone on your team, rest assured that they will demand to see that paradise when the time comes. Fail to deliver that promise, and you will lose integrity. It's critical to maintain core values that will guide you toward your goals, but you can't just speak them: you must live them.

If you ask your team members to work an extra shift, don't go off and nap in the corner office just because you're the boss. People want to see you live your values. You can't preach hard work at board meetings, then spend half your time as the leader doing the bare minimum; doing so will kill your credit as a leader.

If you're just starting out and aspire to climb the ladder, remember that you will still need to work with the people below you. If you're not known for integrity now, it could derail your abilities to motivate others in the future once you do become a leader. The bottom line is this: the key to achieving balance is ensuring that your actions remain in line with your values.

Nobody wants to follow a leader who changes direction like the weather. People love consistency and predictability; they don't want your values to waver according to opinion polls. They want someone who is firm and dependable.

Yes, change is the only constant thing in life, but staying firm in your values doesn't mean that you are rigid. Instead, it only means that your core values must remain the same while you change strategies to fit various situations. Dependability is about values, not tactics.

People connect with leaders with whom they share values, which is also why followers often leave when they find that their leader's values have changed. By helping people feel like they are a part of something greater than themselves alone, your leadership can give followers a vision for their lives, and they'll appreciate you for it. If you have high-flyers on your team, you can celebrate and elevate them as a way of showing your support and how much you value them—but take care to never take credit for the work of others. A true leader goes out of their way to highlight the work of others, without bringing attention to themselves.

Be Accessible

It's common for coworkers to seek you out as a subject matter expert in some situations. Some coworkers may even seek direction for an issue that's unrelated to their jobs, such as personal financial advice. It all depends on what kinds of connections you have built with your colleagues; but to be sought after for your counsel and knowledge—these are the kind of connections you want. You want to be approachable, accessible, and friendly, and you want to create an open environment.

It's always a best practice to have strong interpersonal relationships with the people you work with. Not necessarily deep friendships, but at least strong working relationships in which you appreciate each other as individuals. This means that you must be constantly in learning mode and must remain accessible to others. It's also in your best interest to make sure others know about your learning points, so that you all can develop together.

Communicating, Not Talking

The manner in which you communicate your thoughts to your team and coworkers matters a lot in terms of how they view you, and also in terms of whether you'll attain your goals. If, for example, you are managing a team, it pays to smile a lot, maintain eye contact, and genuinely listen to the opinions of your team members—no matter what education level they've achieved, what position they're in, what their experience or background may be. When you do these things, people feel more open to share their own perspective, and better about themselves as contributors. This, in turn, can lead them to generate better ideas, opinions, and feedback—all of which may be very helpful to you in making better decisions.

As a leader, you should always be present and available to help the entire team achieve its goals. If your team members see you frequently working in the trenches with them, you will earn their admiration and respect. If an employee is talking to you, put down your phone, look away from your computer, and stop shuffling papers. Give them your undivided attention; it will go a long way toward showing how much you respect the opinions of those who work for you.

Help Others

Mahatma Gandhi said, "The best way to find yourself is to lose yourself in the service of others." Leadership is best measured by considering how many people you have helped develop into leaders, or who you've helped become better versions of themselves. And in the course of helping others find themselves, you'll find that serving others will also help you find your own way. Good leaders set aside their own needs when called upon—they show up for the good of others. It's all about sacrificing—be it your money, time, or resources—to help other people meet their goals.

This may appear deceptively easy to achieve, but it's not as straightforward as it seems. You must first place focus on what you want to accomplish and avoid distractions. As a leader, you need to know how to play to the strengths of the individuals in your team. Don't waste time developing their weaknesses—instead, identify the things they excel at already, and help them elevate those attributes from "good" to "great." Their weaknesses just might turn into strengths. Leadership is about building skills that are complementary in nature.

People seek empowerment, and they'll admire you if you're able to show them the way. By empowering those you work with, you minimize the risk of failure and give them room to grow, including the freedom to innovate. They'll strive to ensure that your goals are met because they will see the value in the work.

Empowering team members also breeds respect and trust for you, helping you build powerful relationships where everyone maintains a focus on achieving goals. As a part of this empowerment, it is on you as a leader to maintain constant communication about expectations, milestones, obstacles, and progress reports. Develop strategies that keep everyone engaged and informed of your intentions.

Watch Out for Attitude

Attitude is king. Anyone can be trained in skills, but training for attitude is a bit harder. If you have the opportunity to assemble your own team, choose people who will bring out the best in your leadership efforts; then do all you can to bring out the best in them. Hire great people, set them on the right path, and allow them to do what they've been hired to do.

Lessening your importance in the dynamic can lead to significant gains for the team as a whole. Sometimes, things might not go as planned, but you must press on and be flexible and open to changes as the need arises. Adaptability to changes, situations, and challenges is key: you must constantly evolve to become a better leader.

Treat Everyone Well

None of the tactics I've described will work if you don't take care of your people. When you're hiring, consider a candidate's character right alongside his or her skills. An impressive resume is good, but it's just as important that the potential employee's character fits your goals. Anyone can learn and develop good skills, but good character and attitude are very difficult to achieve. Over the last few years, I have learned from my manager, Bob Kurilko, the importance of hiring based on 3 characteristics: skill, attitude, and cultural contribution. Each one of these is just as important as the next, and by weighing them equally in the interview process, we have hired an exceptional team that thrives in a collaborative environment.

Once you find people who are a good fit for your organization, do everything you can to keep them happy and retain them:

- Provide benefits and help them grow to their full potential.
- Reward top performers.
- Invest heavily in your top 20 percent of talent: train them and develop their leadership skills.

There's an adage that states: "People don't care how much you know until they know how much you care." Follow that adage. Engage by staying tuned in to the people you serve. Leaders listen to and understand their team members, rather than demand and insist on perfection. Put your people first.

Have a Positive Outlook

There are plenty of angry bosses out there who yell and frown at the slightest thing. Some leaders think that being rough and tough will make people work more efficiently, but that's simply not true. A good leader has a positive demeanor and outlook on matters that affect the organization.

Compliment your staff when they do the right thing. Show your appreciation for someone who has done something worthy of commendation, and see how that expression of appreciation will spur other teammates to do good work, too. If you maintain a positive vibe in your team, your employees will rally around you and your vision. They'll trust that you believe in them and their ability to achieve the team's goals.

Empower Staff to Make Decisions

In a small business, it's easy to fall into the trap of being the only one to call the shots. This may give you the impression that you have a firm grip on things; but in fact, it's detrimental to your business. Your subordinates will feel weak and disempowered, like sitting ducks.

The whole point of being a leader is to train others to be so good at their jobs, that if you disappeared completely, the organization will still be able to function effectively. How can you do this? Allow your team to make decisions, while you act as an overseer and an adviser. Even if they make wrong decisions or handle a situation in a way you don't agree with, never chastise them. Instead, use it as a training opportunity. Allow them to share the reasons for their actions before dissecting the situation or suggesting alternatives. If you do, you might better understand and find the logic behind what was done.

Humans are gregarious creatures, so organizations often segment into factions or groups. Sometimes, this segmentation presents problems when it comes to cooperation. To foster good relationships throughout your company, encourage cooperation among all teams and departments. Set up projects so different teams must collaborate to meet the goal, and change up the members of those teams from time to time.

Help People Find Their Purpose

Many people come to work every day looking for validation. They don't just want to be seen and heard, or to be considered important—they want to be taken seriously. Eventually, we all must deal with situations in which the professional lives of other people are in our care. But whether you are a leader or just a regular employee, the truth still remains: people want to be valued, to be useful, and to be treated right.

In a constantly changing workforce, leaders must rethink how they relate to employees all the time, and constantly work to keep teams focused on their goals. You must become more intuitive and resist falling into the trap of following traditional methods of leadership—most of which are very uninspiring. Make efforts to be in touch with the realities of today's workplace, set aside personal agendas, and stay genuinely connected to each and every member of your team. Actively work to inspire them to create their own valuable relationships; these will help them reach their own personal career goals alongside the goals of the team.

A good start: help team members find their purpose. People enter the workforce for many different reasons: money, benefits, personal satisfaction, and so on. But at the end of the day, most people still want their work to matter. Team members will feel more fulfilled if they've found their purpose and are able to act on it. Consider the time you spend with your team as opportunities to help them find their purpose (if they haven't yet done so) and make it clear that you're also eager to help them achieve their career goals.

Words are powerful. It's impossible to tell the reach and impact your counsel may have in propelling your team toward success. If they know that you are looking beyond the immediate goals and are able to visualize a wider-reaching impact, while also helping them achieve their personal milestones, they'll be willing to support you as a leader.

Focus on the Ingredients, Rather than the Recipe

If you want to inspire employees, you must get to know them well. It's human nature to want to spend time with people who understand our tendencies, aptitudes, and behaviors. The very best coaches and leaders always do. How can you inspire someone if you don't know his or her pain points? How can you help inspire others to build an inner circle if you don't know how they connect with others, what their career goals are, and what sorts of situations they thrive in?

Make the time you spend with your team matter. Just being with them without making it count is a waste of your time and theirs.

Nothing about you, including your titles and achievements, matters if people can't hold on to something after you have moved on in your career. The best leaders know their team members so well that the advice they give them—whether it's designed to help them build their networks or discharge their daily activities more efficiently—is well-tailored and suited to their career, and thus much more valuable to them. If the ingredients are better, the recipe will be, too.

Don't Just Lead; Inspire

People usually don't like being told what to do. Most have a strong desire to be relevant, to exercise initiative. When they work for leaders who inspire only fear, they become unproductive. No one likes to be lectured—instead, we long to be coached by leaders who pay attention. In such situations, many of us are much more receptive to objective feedback, as well.

Therefore, it makes sense for leaders to simplify the process of learning. Teach, rather than lecture. There's no point in exhausting everyone with buzzwords they don't understand. Simply communicate the directions, provide the right tools and support, and then get out of the way; let your team members do their jobs. This is being a great teacher and facilitator. People are inspired when they're given the opportunity to learn and then leadership steps aside and lets them do great stuff.

While helping team members become successful is very important, it's not very inspiring in and of itself. People want to get more out of their leaders. If you can help them activate their potential in ways that make them feel more responsible for their careers, you'll do something more significant, something with long-lasting impact. Design your team's performance reviews in ways that highlight their successes and significance. You can't know the impact of someone's performance until you measure it—and only then can you inspire them to greater performance.

Team members who feel respected and valued will always perform better. While appreciation and praise are important, respect is even more so. While everyone wants to be respected, it is up to the leader to establish the rules of how respect is earned.

Every workplace is crawling with recognition addicts, and because we face so much competition there, we often believe that we are our own best allies, that we can only believe in and rely on ourselves. But this belief endangers careers in the long term. If you put too much emphasis on being recognized, you run the risk of deemphasizing the significance of earning respect. If you wish to inspire your team members, train them on the importance of respect and show them how they can earn it. When people see the impact that respect delivers, they'll be motivated by your example.

Historically, leaders have often used a strategy of increasing their employees' responsibility to inspire better performance. Although this approach may have its advantages, it's not usually as effective as when leaders help their team members toward professional growth and development through mentorship.

This mentorship can take the form of encouraging team members to leverage networking opportunities and performance development forums or buying materials and books that can help team members grow and advance in their work. Phil Jackson, a basketball coach who led the Chicago Bulls and Los Angeles Lakers to 11 NBA championships, was known for giving his players books intended to help them become better team members and leaders on the basketball court. These books, including John C. Maxwell's *Developing the Leader Within You* and *Blink* by Malcolm Gladwell, were intended to change the players' way of thinking not only about basketball, but also about leadership and their commitment to others. Jackson believed there is untapped potential in everyone (not just the Kobe Bryants and Michael Jordans of the world), and these books were part of his methodology to help surface these skills.

These methods wouldn't have been successful were it not for the relationships Jackson created with his players. In the end, relationships based on trust inspire teams to perform. These strategies will combine to help foster trust and inspire performance among your own team members, too. When you trust someone, you believe in them, and they can feel it. They're inspired because they know you believe they have what it takes to deliver. Inspiring team members to perform at an optimal level and beyond requires leadership that can see past the obvious. Inspiration isn't a switch that you can turn off and on; rather, it requires consistent behavior aimed at making people feel like they matter and helping them see how much you care about them.

Some people see the work they do on a daily basis as their life's work, and they find happiness and accomplishment in it. They feel that their work is greater than them, and they want it to have a lasting impact. To inspire employees like this, leaders must allow them to innovate and implement their ideas.

Just the process of implementing ideas can be fun and exciting. On that journey, they will likely meet other people with whom they share similar interests, thus allowing them to further grow and bond with their own network, which in turn will inspire them to perform at an even higher level.

It's just as important to provide employees with the tools and resources they need to innovate in their field. If your relationships with your team members are close, you'll know what they need and what resources they require to reach a higher performance level. With access to the right resources and tools, the best of the best can instinctively challenge themselves (that's why incentives are so effective at improving performance). Opportunities to improve individual value help team members grow.

Accountability is very important, of course, but extending ownership to people on a team allows that accountability to be sustained. None of that can happen without a firm foundation of trust and the willpower to go beyond what is deserved. By giving team members a sense of ownership, you are entrusting and sharing your authority with them.

For example, imagine that you've created a special project and asked a team member to take ownership of it. When delegating the ownership, you clearly outline your expectations for what you expect as the end result of the project, including a schedule. As the project proceeds, pay close observation to the team member's attitude and desire to perform. At the end of the project, you can catalog what you've learned about the employee's performance as a means to customize the best approach for inspiring him or her to succeed in the long term.

Inspire others to be successful and build their own strong relationships. If you push your team members to be their very best and follow the steps outlined above, both the team and the individual employees benefit. They will find that more doors are opened to them, they will receive more respect, and the team will work better together toward a unified goal.

CHAPTER EIGHT

ADVISING OTHERS

Once you get the job or position you've long wanted, your goals— and your status—will shift. You will no longer be worried about being stuck at the bottom of the totem pole. Soon, people will start coming to you for advice, both professional and personal, particularly if you have been doing a lot of good work growing your network, organizing professional activities, and showing a sense of purpose in your career.

In this role, maybe you have a team to coordinate and direct or maybe not, but it's still a leadership position in which you can excel or fail. If you're in this position, you must to be able to anticipate some of the challenges that are coming, as your new advice-giving status may evoke a range of emotions. For example, if you tend to be a power freak, a relationship builder, or a know-it-all, all of these tendencies will show up. It may take some time to get the hang of your new role. The following are a few guidelines that may help you navigate these waters successfully.

Know when you're being asked for advice. Most of the time, when people are troubled, they really just want to talk to you about themselves. It's a way to relieve themselves of their emotional burdens or simply to just rant about the situation. Maybe all you'll have to do is simply sit there and listen. When you're in a situation like this, it's tempting to give advice; but many people who think they're being asked for advice in fact are not. Doling out unwanted advice is a character flaw. When people come to you to share their problems, it's wise to ask whether they're seeking your advice before giving it. Regardless of the response, you will both be more comfortable once the question is asked.

Consider whether you're really qualified to give advice on personal matters; it might be best to advise only on professional issues. Most people struggle with giving personal advice, and you might fall into the category of "most people." Thus, you need to make sure of what the issue really is about which your advice is being sought: is it a professional issue? A personal one? A combination of both? Early on in our careers, our problems are often a combination of personal and professional issues (for example, a reluctance to speak up in meetings may be caused by deep-rooted self-esteem issues). Know where your strengths lie, and know what kind of advice you're qualified to give.

Understand the different situations that may lead a person to come to you for advice. You may be asked for advice by a new employee who's transitioning into the workplace from school, or from a previous working environment. In those cases, it's much more useful to give a general orientation to the workplace, versus specific advice on its own. After all, you're the insider.

The biggest challenge in such a situation is remembering how it feels to be clueless, but it's important to do so because it can help both you and the advice-seeker get some perspective on the problem. Do your best to explain, in very plain and concise language, the work environment they're entering and what's going on at that point in time. If there are specific questions—for example, "Is this situation normal or not?" or "Is it possible to do this?"—answer them to the best of your ability.

If you're asked for advice on how to work with certain people, and you're well acquainted with the individuals in question, you may be in a position to help. You could explain to the best of your knowledge what these individuals care about, what concerns they have, what perceptions or misperceptions they might have, what their plans and agendas might be, and so on.

If you're asked to provide guidance, whether it's for step-by-step instructions or about a process you've successfully navigated (such as the organization of a team meeting or company event), first figure out exactly what advice you are being asked for. Confirm your understanding of the request and then advise accordingly.

Know the extent of your expertise. It's always okay to say, "I don't know." You might think it will drum up feelings of insecurity, but that's hardly the case. When you do say that you don't know, it never hurts to add, "My expertise doesn't extend to this, but I think you can probably ask X or Y, and they'll be able to help you." Learn to identify when you're out of ideas and sense the desire to make up an answer welling up inside you. When you're being consulted by someone who respects you, making up an answer is a poor choice. No one can be expected to know everything, so resist the need to fake your way through the conversation. Doing so will harm your credibility.

Be clear about the situation. Before you start issuing advice, be sure that you fully understand the big picture and have your facts straight. The person who seeks your advice and guidance may not even be clear about the nature of the situation, and you may well turn up important facts that change it—for example, in instances where someone comes to you to help restore order to a chaotic situation.

Imagine that a coworker approaches you, briefly describes a situation, and says, "What should I do next to help me learn and succeed here?" First things first: get all the facts straight in order to gain some perspective. Some situations are clear and straightforward, and others aren't. Know when to ask directive questions, which are questions that presuppose you have a firm understanding of the issue and require a specific answer. For example:

- "Have you registered for the certification exam?"

You should also know when to ask semi-directive questions, or questions that are rather vague and designed to keep the person talking so you can figure out what the real issue is. For example:

- "How did you decide to take this particular exam?"

Sometimes, it's helpful to explore different parts of a situation, and sometimes it isn't. Being a leader requires you to know the difference.

Find out why the question is being asked. Often, people don't know how to ask questions; or because they lack a thorough understanding of a situation, they ask the wrong questions. Whether the question is right or wrong, it's usually best to find out what motivated it to begin with. Unless the question and its answer are very clear and straightforward, avoid giving an answer until you get some broad background on what's prompted the person to ask the question.

Know when you're projecting your interests. One common pitfall to avoid is projecting your own interests on people when they come to you for advice. If someone comes to you for direction, foisting your interests on them is one of the worst things you can do. Most people tend to do this subconsciously, so you may not be aware that you're inadvertently manipulating people into your path. If you don't keep an open mind, you may not even be able to see that other paths exist.

You must understand and be comfortable with the fact that some people just don't share the same goals you do. Some simply want to make money, or have a different career plan, or don't like the work you enjoy, or don't want a nine-to-five job. It's entirely possible that the advice-seeker might not have any interest at all in your work or the career path and trajectory you're on.

If you are going to inspire employees to become leaders, forge meaningful relationships, and guide others, you must step outside your own interests and find and articulate the greatness in others. Understand that others can make their lives better and can make tremendous contributions even if they don't choose the path you did. Their own excellent contributions lie somewhere within them, and your job is to help manifest these contributions and inspire excitement about them.

As a first step, find out where their interests lie and help exploit them. Will it be easy? Probably not. But you can be persuasive, and your confidence in them can help them stay on track. You can also help translate their aspirations into the professional world by considering what, based on your experience, may be possible for them professionally. In effect, you're selling them on their own lives.

No matter what the situation may be, never discourage advice-seekers or tell them they won't be able to make it. Your job is not to ruin dreams. Instead, you're charged with helping them figure out how they can make their best contributions to the world and make their lives better.

Avoid sharing too many personal details. It's easy to fall into the trap of using your personal life as an example when advising others. Sometimes, it works, but usually, it doesn't. Telling stories about your life is rarely helpful, except for cases in which the story might help illustrate a challenge the advice-seeker is facing and explain how you surmounted it. In general, it's best to leave your personal life out of it.

There is one other exception: if the advice-seeker is going through a lot of emotional distress, you might make him or her feel better by explaining how you endured a similar situation and are still standing. Just keep it short, and use stories like these only for encouragement. Remember: this isn't about you.

Be nice. Don't be a jerk because someone asked you for advice. Under the pretext of giving "frank advice," some people can be insulting, rude, or obnoxious. Be caring when advising a person who has opened up to you. You don't need to insult someone to get your point across.

Be extra careful when advising a person who is emotionally distraught. Imagine that you're approached for advice by someone who's just lost a job or is about to lose one; has a loved one who's in the hospital, critically ill; or is at risk of losing his or her home. In situations like these, advice-seekers are emotionally upset and may be incapable of rational thought, at least for the moment. It's only human to react this way, and advice-seekers shouldn't be blamed for it.

Instead, accommodate the situation by asking them to effectively pause the situation, and to not do anything that demands rational thought until they're in a better place emotionally. Don't fall over yourself explaining things or telling them you know how they feel. You probably don't. Just listen, and when the time comes for you to talk, simply restate the facts of the situation as they've been explained to you—showing that you're truly listening—and don't try to evaluate or change them. This is the first step to reestablishing a rational, concrete thinking process.

As you listen, be on the lookout for instances where the facts are blurred with unclear language. Pay attention to any attempts to conflate situations that aren't logically related into distressing emotions, or for attempts to fuse simple, fact-based statements with judgments about what the facts imply. These are ways that distressed people attempt to defy reality. It may or may not be necessary for the person to get realistic about the situation at that moment in time, but in most cases, that's not your decision to make.

If it does seem that the time has come to have a reasonable discussion about the situation, then you can try to keep the conversation on a rational track. Prioritize the issues by asking questions that require the advice-seeker to distinguish between what needs to be dealt with immediately and what can wait for later. Don't pay attention to facts that have no bearing on the current situation. Once you're able to establish a rational line of discussion, you can apply the strategies that have been discussed.

Be conscious of your words—as well as theirs. Those who come to you seeking direction will use their own words to explain their dilemma. But this might create problems, because their words may be unfamiliar to you, or may carry a different meaning. For example, if a mentee says to you, "I had thought this job was going to be meaningful to my life," you might be tempted to agree and take control of the person's words by sympathizing. Resist this urge. Don't presuppose that you understand what's meant unless it's very explicit, and don't try to impose your own meaning on the other person's words. That's a fast way to kill communication. Instead, ask clarifying questions, like, "What do you mean by *meaningful?*" Assume nothing, and always ensure you get the clearest possible picture of the situation.

Be clear about what you know and what you don't. It is good practice to always rephrase what the advice-seeker says to you in your own words and then ask for confirmation. For example, in the above situation, you might reply, "So you're saying that this position has not been meaningful to you because you haven't been promoted in the last three years. Is that correct?" This ensures that you're both on the same page. You don't have a magical power to discern what other people are thinking; asking for confirmation shows that you understand your limitations.

Be aware of your own feelings. Imagine that an advice-seeker is telling you about his or her problems, and suddenly you begin to feel strong emotions, like anger and sadness, as a result of the tale. Or maybe you're just itching to leave the room. Pay attention to these feelings—which may be harder than it sounds.

The first step is becoming aware of the feelings as they happen. Ask yourself: Am I angry? Am I raising my voice? If the answer to the second question is "yes," not only are you experiencing the emotion, you're also acting on it.

Next, proceed by asking yourself further questions:

- **Who does this feeling belong to?** It's common to sympathetically "feel" the advice-seeker's emotions instead of your own, particularly confusion. This is due to one of two factors: natural empathy, or the projection of the advice-seeker's feelings onto you. When you feel emotions while giving advice to someone, stop to figure out if the emotion is truly yours.

- **Is this feeling rational?** Why are you sad, angry, confused, etc.? Is the feeling caused by the present situation you're being made aware of, or has it provoked an emotional wound you've been carrying around? For instance, if you are advising someone who feels oppressed by his or her boss, the situation might bring up memories of your own unresolved experiences of oppression at the hands of your own previous (or even current) bosses, resulting in anger. Dissociate your personal feelings from the current situation, and deal with them later on. Launching into an emotional tirade each time someone comes to you for advice isn't useful to the advice-seeker, or to you. Unless you have extensive training, avoid psychological discussions as well. Simply identifying the feeling, and its source, will make you less likely to act on it.

Know whether the situation requires you to give specific instructions. Spoiler alert: most of the time, it doesn't. We all have different paths, and you're in no position to dictate exactly what path is right for another person, even if you know that person well. If you don't come to terms with this reality, you'll end up committed to offering the only solution that occurs to you. Sometimes, advice-seekers are only looking for reactions or reassurance that that they're not delusional, rather than advice. They may just need a little perspective. In the end, they'll have to figure things out themselves. For your part, figure out what people really want when they come to talk to you before you begin to dispense advice.

Stop if you suspect a hidden agenda. Some people only come to you for advice so they can blame you later. Others pretend to need your advice so they can later resist it. Still others come to you to prove that they're right and someone else is wrong. If you suspect a hidden agenda, don't participate. Most people with a hidden agenda won't own up to it, and it won't do you much good to accuse them of anything. If you feel your time is not being well used, it's best to say that you don't know how to help them and let them go.

Avoid the temptation to pressure, argue, or manipulate. Stating your views is important, of course, but avoid the temptation to argue with, control, or manipulate your advice-seekers. People are responsible for their own actions and must make their own decisions in the end. It's fine to provide them with factual information, but trying to control them will do you (and them) no good.

If the decision the advice-seeker is consulting you about directly affects you, you're not giving out advice; you're negotiating. A good example would be someone asking for advice regarding a project you're both working on in which a conflict of interest exists. If you're negotiating, that must be clear to everyone, including the advice-seeker.

Advice-giving is an iterative process. Sometimes, the advice you give simply won't work, perhaps due to the existence of other facts or information you were unaware of. That's fine. If the advice-seeker re-approaches you, start another round of clarifying the situation. Once you see that advice is an iterative process, you'll be able to frame your guidance in a better way, such as, "Why don't you try this?" or "Have you tried that?"

Deliver your advice in short sessions. No one likes long speeches. If those who you advise resist or make comments while you're talking, they're probably not really listening —and it could be because you're doing all the talking. If they really want to talk, let them do the talking. Think of yourself as simply helping them paint a picture, and let them figure out the process and the thinking on their own. The picture you're painting need not be seamless. As you give advice, frequently ask, "Is this making sense?" to ensure that you are on the same page. Remember to keep it short and keep it simple.

Get to the point quickly. See above. Don't wax philosophical or drone on endlessly. If you have to use an abstract concept to explain something, let the advice-seeker know this and stay focused on the problem. Then, concisely explain your thought process.

Ask only the questions for which you want answers. There is no point in asking questions you already know the answers to. On the other hand, trying to make someone read your mind makes no sense, either. Instead, get comfortable with the idea of asking targeted questions about which you're genuinely curious. For example, if you see others who are making strides in their career, figure out what they're doing right by asking lots of questions. Then, peruse the strategies they share with you—you never know how one of them might be of great help to you or someone else.

If you find yourself giving out the same advice over and over again, it might be helpful to just write it down (which is why I am writing this book). This happens if you're in a position where you work with lots of people who are in the same situation (for example, you're in HR and are constantly asked questions by new hires). If you write down your advice and share it widely, even the people who would never ask for it (but still need it) will benefit.

EPILOGUE

During the past fifteen-plus years of my professional life, I've been fortunate enough to cross paths with some of the best and brightest in my field. Throughout the years, I've come to understand the importance of these relationships. Doors have been opened, introductions have been made, and business opportunities have been created for me—all by virtue of a close network of trusted confidants. But coming to understand what it would take to build and sustain these relationships was not a quick process; it is a skill that took years to come about, and one that takes constant application and refinement as the world around us continues to change. When I began my professional career, there was no social media to leverage and no phone apps to keep us in contact all the time. As the world (and technology) has evolved, so has the foundation upon which relationships lie.

If this book leaves you with any lasting impression, let it be this: relationships are a vital part of career growth and success. While it's important to have a robust network of contacts, the quantity of relationships you have matters far less than their quality. Find those people who you can trust, who push you to improve, and who serve as sounding boards for your ideas, and bring them into your inner circle. These are the people who will advocate for you, even when you're not in the room. They will be your cheerleaders, your support system, and your spokespeople. They will play a role in advancing your professional profile.

In these pages, I've walked through various tactics and methodologies for both building connections such as these and maintaining them in the long term. As I have learned (in some cases, the hard way), nothing can end a relationship faster than only reaching out when you need something. You must maintain your relationships over time, which means reaching out when you have no agenda or favor to ask. Staying connected with your inner circle is a great way to keep your pulse on what business opportunities may be out there, what trends in the marketplace are shifting, and so on. Stay close and connected to your inner network, or it soon may disappear.

Finally, remember that relationships are a two-way street. You need to put just as much into the relationships you forge as you expect to get out of them. Dale Carnegie once said, "You can make more friends in two months by becoming interested in other people than you can in two years by trying to get other people interested in you." Carnegie's words are true for business connections as well. When you have valuable, trust-based connections with the members of your inner circle, the bonds will stay strong. Work hard to ensure you always hold up your side of the relationship.

I have learned a lot in my professional life, including how to be a better employee, a better leader, a better communicator, and beyond. With each and every one of these skills, it was clear to me what value it would bring and why it was so important to develop it. But the one skill I wish I had developed earlier in my career wasn't simply understanding the value of relationships, but instead discerning the difference between distant connections and inner circles.

In the past few years, I've deployed the skills outlined in this book, and it's completely changed the way I interact with those I meet in professional circles. It's also led to bigger and better career opportunities. I encourage everyone to examine their own connections and determine which relationships they value the most. Find the ones that can help you achieve your personal or professional goals and put the skills described here to good use. You'll whittle your wide range of connections down to a close-knit group of confidants and supporters, and the energy you invest in creating your circle will pay dividends.